POTENTIAL

collection of work-life stories

POTENTIAL

collection of work-life stories

Modern Workplace

and

IIoT Smarts

Greg Lush

LMWS | 2018

LMWS books may be purchased for educational, business, or sales promotional use. For information, please email: greglush@lastmileworkersolutions.com

FIRST EDITION: 2018

ISBN 978-0-359-14151-7

LMWS
31 Promontory
Dove Canyon, CA, 92679

www.lastmileworkersolutions.com

ISBN 978-0-359-14151-7

To Dad (Legendary Lee)

Your insights continue to inspire me, rest in peace

Contents

Acknowledgements

Experience, once bottled, must be shared. My career is, and has been, an exploration of what could be. Innovation is a team sport and special thanks to those who have influenced my journey (naming just a few)

Al Jones

Annie Lush

Bob Lake

Charlie Fletcher

Dave Brockway

Dave Whaley

IMG team

Jeff Lush

Lee Lush

Mike Latham

Mike Madison

Ron Wall

Tracy Price

Foreword

By Greg Lush

Even prior to starting my career (1981) I knew that I would follow in my Father's footsteps. I have always had a hunger to help others find solutions, my first exposure started as a field technician. As technology began to permeate our everyday lives, I transitioned to solutions through the application of technology. Many of us, assumed the roles of un-official shepherds, helping guide the Internet into the business world. We were just starting to enjoy our break through with the fax machine, we started experimenting with these things called web pages through our lightning fast 28 baud telephone modems.

Technology paths can be quite different, mine was not IT, but instead helping improve business outcomes through technology (applications). Over the years I evolved into the guy always interested in change, pushing the edges of the envelope, and inventing ways to differentiate organizations in their marketplaces. At first it seemed like the consumers of these tools were so desperate for technology that they were willing to modify the way they worked just to have the opportunity to use these new-fangled software applications. How the times have changed, today's business worker is coming to work with more powerful and user-friendly tools, many times at VERY low cost, and eclipsing the organizational tools provided.

For years I have wanted to collect my experiences, failures and successes and share them with others.

However, we all know how that tune plays, never enough time in the day. Then, four years ago I was invited to receive an award on behalf of my father from Local 250 here in Los Angeles. The conversations with people in our trade, most of whom I had never met before, sharing with me the ways in which my father influenced their lives. How my father, who is the only character in these stories that ties back to a real person (Legendary Lee), helped shape our industry and made it better for all. In that bittersweet moment I decided to move forward in organizing these short stories.

Throughout these stories you will see that I use a handful of characters. It is important to see the stories from all sides; especially in today's environment as the successful use of technology needs to weave in all perspectives. These characters are not the point of the story, instead they are designed to illustrate different opinions and attitudes. The name of the book "POTENTIAL" is appropriate as the challenges to changing business outcomes today have much less to do with technology and so much to do with people. Two "trend" chapters have been released with the first version, modern workplace and IIot Smarts. These chapters, and the stories within, are well suited for all interested parties. None of the content gets technical, instead they are written to get you thinking about things differently, please approach with an open mind. At the end of each story I have included a morale and a few suggested actions.

It is my sincere hope that these stories will help you to deepen the levels of productivity, satisfaction, empowerment, and efficiencies you should be realizing as a result of digital tools. Unfortunately, the reality for some of you may be that you will use the "new" tool in the same manner as before, stymied by your experience.   I implore you to challenge your organization to answer this question; have you replaced your employees Schwinn bicycles with a modern Ford F150 and discovered they only drive on bike paths?

Modern Workplace
Apprehensive Adopter

seeking personal process alignment

The words, modern and workplace are simple enough to understand; however, when combined as modern workplace, what does that mean? For me it almost feels like a "fad" name; you remember these; synergy, green, and countless others... On the following pages you will enjoy a handful of short stories, each with their own moral and thoughts on how to get started on your own journey.

A "Modern Workplace" is whatever you think it should be. Digital tools have evolved to a collection of functions wrapped up in small applications. Think of these functions as bricks lining your own digital transformation path. For many of us this sounds great, you mean we are no longer adjusting our work processes to the constraints of the software? Oh crap, if you are not dictating my path then I need to come up with my own? Here lies the rub as we all transition to the modern workplace and are challenged with answering the question of "why" as opposed to in the past enduring the "what" and "how". Our first story begins:

Finally, we received approval to move to a new platform, security, cloud apprehension and how

to manage financially were all behind us, at least for now. Our immediate action was to socialize our digital transformation plans and get ready for the first of January. Our first story begins with Natalie Naysayer at the kickoff meeting:

As folks assembled in the meeting room you could feel the uneasiness in the air. The invitation read "manage yourself and your clients digitally" with the body of the message including words like "revolutionary and efficient". Although the ground was flat, I was looking for something to trip on, help me fall suddenly and smack my head against the floor, anything to get out of this meeting. You could see the attendees all preparing to take their stance, some were curious and sincerely interested in change, a handful had no real feelings either way, and of course my fellow naysayers. If we added enough resistance to this movement it would fade away like so many others before I thought. Our naysayer silently continues to vent; "the fact of the matter, at least from my perspective, is that I have been successful for years why should I change? If my Big Chief tablet and a number two pencil has worked, let's not upset the apple cart". However, my funk was broken when I heard the first words from the speakers' mouth "I am not here to teach you what or how, instead let's focus on why". These three simple letters threw a curve ball, disrupting my normally aloof responses and attitude.

The speaker continues; "for most it is as simple as helping an individual find the quickest path to their "aha" moment, once discovered all of the resistance will melt away. Modern software development practices and toolsets have made the user experiences and interfaces extremely intuitive. Instead the struggle for most is determining the best way to blend the proposed, and often digital process, into their own successful habits".

This speaker might be making sense, could it be that I may have to retire my naysayer persona? Since my boss will be in the training and Frank, my competition for the next promotion, I will be a bit guarded with my questions. How does that saying go...? be quiet and let people think you are an idiot, open your mouth and prove it. Who makes up these sayings anyhow?

The trick is, as our speaker continues, is to allow your mind to open itself to listening, without bias what the solution provides. Individually begin to connect your thoughts with the routines suggested to gain alignment. Each of you have a journey ahead of you and the steepest climb is getting yourself to the "aha" moment. For now you will probably have to permit yourselves to press the "I believe" button. This blind confidence will serve as your fuel to get you over the aha-hump. So during this session ask questions which get you closer to your personal process alignment. Don't worry about asking questions regarding how the tool functions, that will come after you wrap your head around why this tool is important to you and you alone.

Natalie, drifted off in thought, no longer concerned about how others would perceive the speed in which I was going to "get it", instead questions flowed from my head to the notebook in front of me. These questions, while they may relate to others in the room, were all about me, I could ask them without fear of any comprise to my station within the organization. What a relief, all I need to focus on now is an open mind....

Moral:

Dictated change feels onerous and overwhelming; with my own reflection, resolve and growth is most certainly liberating (Greg Lush)

Start NOW

- Personal effort spent reflecting on how you personally can become more efficient, will pay off in spades

- Shed the burden of thinking about your needs in terms of what the technology can provide, that is so "early 2000's". Instead focus on what you need, in your words and let the digital transformation expert make the alignment to the digital tools

- Organize your needs into categories and weights, consider; client impact, revenue impact, risk (or safety depending on your position); personal impact (quality of work life); curiosity; growth

- Dream BIG, the sky is the limit! Freeing your mind from assumed constraints is critical, wipe "I'm sure it can't do that" from your thoughts. Pull your inner child out who was never afraid to ask "why", repeatedly.

- Schedule coaching sessions with your personal digital coach and / or bring your list to any transformation training or meeting

Modern Workplace
String on Finger

staying digitally organized

Andy thought for sure that the honeymoon period would last longer.... we need to throw the users a bone and get them using the tools as a natural extension of their current habits. What does everyone have in common? Sure, who hasn't had something slip through the cracks? Just last week Chris shared with me his experience, this would be a suitable place to continue our journey; move from stings on our fingers to anxiety-free digital tools:

Chaotic Chris had endured many a tongue lashing in his day but this one would take the prize. As he stood there, focused on the words erupting from his customers' mouth, he concentrated on making sure that the expression on his face showed pure empathy. What a dumbass, all I had to do was put a note in my calendar or better yet send the customer a meeting invitation. Chris began to reflect on why he failed at such a simple task, surely it was because he was just too busy. You know, a star salesman like himself, doesn't have time for the trivial things. Unfortunately, his lack of discipline, arrogance, self-centered attitude, and dis-respect for others... has lost him a key customer.

As Chris drove home that evening, sitting in the endless traffic, his mind began to wander. Could it be that this one incident was not isolated, instead one of many examples in an extensive list of missed activities? Just two weeks ago his boss, Frazzled Frank, simply showed up in his office expecting Chris to have a meaningful conversation regarding his sales pipeline. Chris recalled his feelings at that moment, frustration, anxiety, even a bit of disappointment that Frank had so little respect for Chris's time. Oh my, how horrible, is it possible that those around me are thinking these same things? No way, I am revered in this organization and with my customers, everyone loves me, my personality and relationships make up for my careless behavior, they all accept me as a scatterbrain.

The next morning, tired from a sleepless night, Chris could not escape that pit in his stomach. Normally Chris believed that he was responsible for filling a room with energy, could it be that he was pulling the energy from others? Instead of his normal barrage of pleasantries, he asked Janet about their relationship, specifically how she felt. Juxtaposed Janet, always poised and respectful, simply replied "everything is good Chris", what's on your mind? It was like confessional in some ways, Chris's mind placed a dark veil over Janet and the questions started to flow from his mouth with ease. Janet, as Chris began to blend commentary with questions, he asked "do you believe I appreciate and respect you as a coworker"? An expression flooded Janet's face, one that Chris had never seen before, she was perplexed. Noticing the discomfort in the questioning Chris pleaded that Janet speak her mind.

Janet began to share her thoughts with Chris. When we spend time with one another I am filled with appreciation for our working relationship, she started, I wish we had more of those face to face experiences. Unfortunately, once you are away something happens, it is as if you believe that your time is more important than everyone else's. It makes me, fellow workers, and customers feel that we should be fortunate if you choose to keep an appointment or follow up on a commitment, Janet explained. Oh my, I am a real jackass thought Chris as Janet continued to share her honest feedback. Chris listened intently, absorbing these words filled with honesty and the best intentions.

A few weeks later Reluctant Ruth was watching Chris enter the coffee shop for their morning meeting and noticed his relaxed aura. Chris, did you just return from vacation, asked Ruth. No, you would not believe me if I told you. Ruth, you know how reluctant you are to try new things, if it isn't broke why fix it? Chris continued as Ruth shook her head in acknowledgement, well... here it is, I started using a digital calendar to manage my time and a tasking tool to keep track of commitments that I need to complete. In pure disbelief Ruth could only say, really? Yes, you would be amazed at how much less chaotic my days have been since I decided to move to digital organization systems. It is really something Ruth, before my days were filled with large gaps and the meetings I had with people were less productive. Now, with everyone in the know, we are focused and look forward to our time together. Just as a bonus, commitments so often made during meetings, do not fall through the cracks as they have for so many years. I am relaxed, my teammates and clients are happier, and I have no more anxiety regarding what I may have forgotten to accomplish. For me it took a negative event to get me headed in the right direction, everyone is different; however, I encourage you to find the reason why and take the first step yourself. When you look back you will wonder what it was that held you back in the first place. Now, enough talk let's get breakfast ordered; on to those waffles!

Moral:

Don't let your perceptions blind you to the reality that surrounds your every action (Greg Lush)

Start NOW

- Define the difference between a reminder and a task. For me, reminders are quick memory nudges and take minutes to disposition or complete. Tasks are always tied to a customer, initiative, project, etc. and generally vary in length from 15 minutes to hours

- Many tools incorporate reminder-based tools, choose the tool which you use most frequently from the largest variety of locations

- Habits are HARD to start, yet once every day if you set a digital reminder for yourself you will be amazed how quickly your dependency grows

- Take the first step and move from paper-based reminders, sticky notes, etc. over to a digital tool. For me the criteria for my first digital reminder tool is something that is easy to fill out, reminds me automatically, and can be used across all computing mediums.

- Using your calendar for managing reminders... A very common approach and works well if you do not have many meetings. However, my preference is to keep things in context, calendar for appointments and reminders for ticklers.

Modern Workplace
Eternal Experts

leveraging knowledge-based bots

How does that saying go? Out with the old and in with the new? Certainly, one could relate this to individuals and digital tools. Yet it was time to say goodbye to a fellow worker, a friend for many years. How would we make sure that his know-how was passed on and shared within the organization? Our story picks up as Andy drives into work...

My mind drifted as I drove in to work on this perfect day. The sun was shining, birds were chirping, and traffic was flowing smoothly. I tried to imagine what work would be like after the retirement party for Legendary Lee, a fountain of knowledge for all of us over the past two decades. Lee was involved or led change for the organization; touching everything from internal systems and tools to external innovations to help differentiate us with our customers. When I was 17 my Father reminded me that nobody was irreplaceable yet on this day I struggled with how questions would be answered tomorrow and who or what would fill this "knowledge void".

As I pulled into the parking lot Influential Irene was sitting in her car, her eyes a bit swollen as if she had been crying. When I was having a tough day, it was Irene who I went to see, she always had this infectious smile that could brighten anyone's day. Today was different, Irene was close Lee, and it was obvious that his retirement was taking a toll. She is not quite ready to go inside I thought to myself, so I gently tapped on her cars passenger window, hoping that some of my good cheer from this morning would rub off on her. The door unlocked and in a shaking voice Irene said, please join me Andy. While I am not the sharpest tool in the shed, two decades of marriage taught me to not say much, just make sure that Irene knew I was there for her if she felt like talking. As I made my way into the passenger's seat I leaned over saying, "Lee had a great run".

He is just retiring for crying out loud, I'm not sure why this if affecting me in this way. Irene continued, Lee and I have been preparing months for this day. Desperate to shift the conversation to the future, I said "what do you mean by your comment preparing months"? Irene continued; relevant and immediate access to information, unstructured antidotes and structed knowledge sources, have always been a challenge. Unstructured antidotes, or what Lee often called "tribal knowledge" is by far the hardest knowledge to share to a broad audience, this information is generally obtained by having a relationship with the person in the know. Structured knowledge is plentiful, you know those files, presentations, etc. passed out during training and stored in the digital "knowledge library". Both types of information require requestors to ask the question in exactly the proper way or the results will be inconsistent. Andy could see that his curiosity was starting to lift Irene's spirits, "Irene very interesting, please tell me more".

Over the years Lee had become increasingly frustrated with the ability to influence and in many cases, convince others that the proposed change would be beneficial. If all the stars aligned, and everyone could make the connection to their daily routines, we would be in great shape. However, the last few years increase in opportunities to use new tools, and the almost endless updates and shifts to better tools, have left consumers in a constant state of flux. Lee knew that our traditional means of communicating and managing knowledge had to adapt to the times or the users would become increasingly frustrated. About six months ago Lee had a great idea, continued Irene, we need to create an environment where you could ask, in your own words and style, stream of consciousness questions. This approach, thought Lee, would be a way in which he could share his knowledge long after retirement. Irene recalled, just as Lee was getting me on board with the concept he proclaimed, "and we will do this with a Conversational BOT"! What? A BOT seemed a bit outrageous, wasn't it easier to deploy incremental change and not disruptive change Irene fired back to Lee. Absolutely, Lee stated in his reassuring and confident manner, yet we will never meet our objective of everyone being continuously informed.

So, Lee and I began our research. We discovered that these bots (computer-based logical routines and conversational threads) are operating all around us. Sometimes people confuse these bots with sophisticated search algorithms, this is not the area that had any interest to Lee. Instead, the bot, in his mind, can be used to take advantage of and make meaningful the correlation between a multitude of digital systems. These systems can reside either within or outside of your computing environments. One of the greatest advantages, which struck me immediately, was the ability to simply carry on a conversation with a person, using natural language. In the background, predicting and guiding the human through bot-based responses. Why should anyone be concerned with what system they must enter this... or go to find that? As we begin to explore the technology, this humanistic conversation-based approach, it dawned on us that the possibilities were endless. These underlying algorithms and machine learning routines would consume knowledge and make it available at any time to any person. You could hear a change in Irene's voice, she realized that today would be bittersweet, Lee's retirement and the release of his replacement, OurBOT. Computer based BOTs can manage elevated levels of connections in ways that humans cannot; however, make no mistake they will never replace any human. The swelling in Irene's eyes had diminished and it was time to head inside, we have a retirement party to attend!

Moral:

Experiential knowledge is just a tall-tale until properly channeled to a consumable medium (Greg Lush)

Start NOW:

- Regardless of digital toolset, identify mechanisms for capturing institutional knowledge. Remember that you eat an elephant one bite at a time

- Do not procrastinate, you can lay out a strategy for minding to the information within your organization, just take the first step

- BOT's at their simplest level are based on question and answer pairings, start an FAQ NOW if you are not quite ready to begin with BOT development

- Initiate a cross-department team, "our legacy" and begin meeting on a regular basis to identify key individuals and the tactics to interview, extract and distribute these nuggets of knowledge-based gold

Modern Workplace
Differentiator or Detractor

are you stuck in place?

We are getting in a groove with our medium-sized branch, does that mean we can apply the same recipe to all branches? Fingers were crossed behind Franks back as he pondered that possibility. Unfortunately, our story picks up in a slightly different spot:

Could it be that "best intentions" would not be enough to chip through the hardened exterior of this organizations habits, thought Frustrated Frank. As the digital transformation honeymoon period slipped into the rear-view mirror, the burden of change seemed to settle into place.

Frank, it is no longer about the tools, instead it is each person's rationalization of why these tools will make them stronger; habits are challenging, continued Andy. On one hand, if it works why fix it, and the other hand growth requires continuous innovation. The organizational structure has an impact, flat organizations require compelling reasons to change. For instance, significant pain points within the business resulting in lost revenue, market or corporate dictated edicts. Without these, change lacks a sense of urgency and is at the discretion of the local management, the larger the operation, the greater the number of management layers, the higher probability of lackluster adoption.

Often, larger branches; flush with sales and work are focused acutely on execution and elect to defer change. Whereas the smaller branches are always seeking an edge, they do not have the momentum of the larger branch. Thus, adoption and use of new tools are welcomed as clear differentiators, as opposed to perceived distractors. The approach may also be different; those with high work volume may not want to see and assess options, instead simply receive training; small branches may want a stronger "consultative" approach, plant the seed and help it grow. These behaviors may also be observed from department to department within a branch. In 2018, the people component is the largest contributor or detractor influencing successful adoption. Thanks, said Frank, your perspectives have provided me with fresh ideas.

Innovation flourishes in communities were individuals are encouraged to challenge the norm and direction. At what point is it appropriate to say, we have chosen a path and will stick with it, where is the balance between empowerment and leadership? Managing polarization and moving beyond the rhetorical simplicity of prioritizing one value over all others or a false-choice narrative that freezes action-oriented debate into prolonged indecision. You are either on the gas or the brakes, winning has no room for those simply coasting. How are you driving sustainable adoption?

Moral:

Whether you believe you can, or you can't, you are right (Henry Ford)

Start NOW:

- Timing is everything, especially with the larger branches

- The deeper the management, the tougher the climb. Introducing tools, slow and steady allow middle managers to get their arms around the tools BEFORE the general population.

- It is very important that folks in management and leadership roles are never asked questions regarding new tools that they cannot help those asking (directly or indirectly)

- Visualizing progress and getting commitments and timing from branch managers helps tremendously. Everyone is "in the loop", always.

Modern Workplace
Digital Coaches

empathy in action

Is it too much for me to endure? The idea of making a disruptive change and rocking the very core of what we have done for years is a bit unsettling. What happens if I need some hand-holding? If you close your eyes you can almost imagine the sweat building on Oscar's brow as he contemplated his last step through the door of the Modern Workplace. Our final story provides a light at the end of the tunnel, read on...

It had to be about halfway through my drive into work that I began to feel a throbbing pain in my forearms and hands. I was clutching the steering wheel so tightly as the anxiety continued to build regarding the changes happening at the office this morning. So, I decided, like any red blooded American, to search my iPod (2007 model) for the quintessential song to help me through this moment; "Eye of the Tiger" by the appropriately named band Survivor. Even I, Overwhelmed Oscar, can muster the strength to get through our companies transition to the cloud, I repeated to myself while listening to this song repeatedly.

Influential Irene and I were "cube-mates", I began to share some of my thoughts with her hoping it would relieve some of my stress. Irene, "from a technology perspective, things seemed so much simpler in the late 90s and early 2000's. We all consumed and learned how to leverage software packages, institutionally installed and likely to remain in service for many years. Admittedly the flexibility of the software tools was quite limited; however, we learned to adapt our workflow processes to those supported within the solutions provided." Irene added "the training regiments were straightforward as well, we prepared content, delivered during a training class, and monitored results."

So, Oscar, continued Irene, "why are you so anxious?" The question was so simple, yet Oscar was struggling to put together a response. Initially Oscar began to realize the silliness of his anxiety, heck this is just a different software system, it serves the same function, why am I getting so upset? I just need to "rise to the challenge" as I hummed the song now burned into my prefrontal cortex. I have it Irene, proclaimed Oscar; "the difference is the paths we have to take are now much greater than they were in the past". For instance, when I come up to T intersection just two choices are available, left or right. Yet this cloud-based solution is more like a city center where I can drive in one spoke and am presented with 15 alternate routes. The choices are so robust that I struggle with where to start, in the past these decisions were made on my behalf.

Irene, who was responsible for training in the organization, transitioned quickly through two emotions; enlightenment and concern. Enlightenment as she agreed with Oscars response and concern as the traditional training approaches for software packages would not work in delivering cloud-based solutions. The same core elements for adoption had to be in place, the user had to resolve to use the tool, and the leadership had to provide clear expectations. But it was more than that, company level training needed to cover how to get to the toolset, individual and team coaching would position the software as a benefit and not just another distraction. Time would be spent understanding the natural work habits of an individual and suggesting a path to productivity. The real beauty, thought Irene, was the flexibility of a standard platform which could be personalized, without customization or compromise of corporate objectives, to each person.

It is not hard to find articles talking about digital transformation yet very few speak to the need for digital coaching. Providing a one-size-fits-all approach will likely yield the same or even reduced use of tools as the user will never think to stretch outside of their comfort zones. If the objective is to enrich the user's experience with this transition, you will have to put time into developing digital coaching approaches.

Moral:

The paradox of choice often leaves us anxious and finding comfort in denial, ignorance and loss of perspective (Greg Lush)

Start NOW:

- Every individual will deal with change in a unique way, providing a coaching resource, regardless of whether it is leveraged or not, will calm many

- As folks become more comfortable they will find themselves asking the question, "I wonder if it could do..."; however, conflicted as they will not have the time or background to establish which tool to use. Digital Coaching, with a solid consulting type approach, will increase adoption exponentially

- You should be constantly "building a bench" of those seeking coaching and flipping them into those providing coaching. Individual elements learned by one person can always be shared with many.

Modern Workplace
Conclusion

Embracing the modern workplace across an organization is not an easy task. The good news is that the tools have become very stable, affordable, and readily available. The more challenging news is that successful adoption of the modern workplace requires massive cultural change. Most of the tools today, regardless of platform, will suggest that you not simply change email programs but instead re-consider the way that you compute. Modern workplace platforms were designed to be inclusive, ask you to connect numerous systems, and think about knowledge in context of what you are doing. For instance, if you execute projects; your context may be with those projects and / or clients. If I searched for information regarding ABC client I should see everything, in one spot, about ABC. No longer do I care that the social feed is coming through an AI tool, their market conditions from another micro-service, transactional information from our company. It should all be in context, what myself and others like to refer to as the age of "contextual computing". The value you extract from your modern workplace tools is all in your own hands, dare to dream and dream BIG as the digital world is yours for the taking. Do amazing things for your clients, your employees and your positive impact on the places we live and love.

Intentionally left blank

Ditch the shotgun

laser focus when considering IIoT

Several months have passed as we rejoin our digital transformation journey. The office, field workers and our customers are all enjoying a renewed sense of communication. How refreshing that the modern workplace has changed the way that we look at computing. Our characters are now positioning themselves to attack the world of intelligence, perspective and 21st century approaches to extending the life of equipment, increasing resilience, and saving money. Let's pick up the story and jump into the Industrial Internet of Things (IIoT). PS: these are NOT technical stories and written with all readers in mind.... enjoy!

Now this is really a great presentation thought influential Irene as she hung on every word of this riveting discussion on the Industrial Internet of Things (IIoT). As the message continued she didn't feel as though she was being pulled into a rabbit hole but instead as if she was being introduced to the universe. This euphoric feeling reminded her of the days she spent staring at the lava lamp while being completely immersed in the sounds of Pink Floyd. A bit dazed but loving every minute... if we could pull off this fabric of sensors and actuators, combined with previously isolated information around worker metrics, financial results, weather conditions; we would have a significant impact.

While the technology was sophisticated, it was quite straightforward. Our biggest challenge will be figuring out exactly what we need to do in a scope which was digestible. Irene knew that our results would fund future expansion of these new SMART business applications.

Irene went into work the next day high on enthusiasm and couldn't wait to share her experiences with others in the office. Each time she spoke with someone, new possibilities arose, at the end of the morning she was starting to feel a lot like how Overwhelmed Oscar must feel daily. The last person Irene shared the news with was Avid Andy. Andy asked Irene, it appears that opportunity is everywhere, what are your thoughts on how to boil this down to one or two meaningful use cases? Irene's euphoria was certainly grounded now. Getting excited was one thing, understanding the technology another, but focusing in on our targets would take a different approach than in the past.

Andy could sense that Irene was a bit perplexed. We need to change the way we look at this Irene, said Andy to get her back on track. For years we have dealt with enterprise systems and in many instances focused on "what and how", impressing folks with a list of capabilities and features. We would even bang the "fully integrated" drum if we were really feeling cocky. Instead, continued Andy, we must flip this inside-out and focus sharply on "why". For instance, let's say that we were a vending machine service company, and our job was to understand what people liked and make sure the product was always available. Our use case might be; "stocked and always satisfying", sensors would help us understand inventory levels, and machine learning would direct us on which items were being selected more than others, on which days, and possibly even by whom. While this may seem simplistic, and ridiculously obvious, enormous potential exists to save on labor, lost inventory from theft and expiration, and retained contracts as the consumers are always getting exactly what they want.

Andy could see the tension rolling off Irene's shoulders. It is easy to get caught up with all the exciting products; however, slow and steady will win this race. What was that story about the tortoise and hare? Irene was certainly not an egomaniac; however, she would be the first to admit that starting with the IIOT approach on such a simple task may not be filled with the glory of other use cases. Yet Irene knew that it is much easier to grab the low hanging fruit. I will begin tomorrow aggregating all our ideas, cross reference them to one another, and find the one or two use cases which make the most business sense. Off to the races!

Moral:

Crawl. Walk. Run. (Tracy Price)

Start NOW:

- Forget about the technology and focus on what differentiates you in the market

- Be extremely pragmatic when selecting your first use case, first mover advantage in this immature market, will hinge on both perception and reality

- Your team must be diverse, the best solutions to problems must come from those dealing with the equipment on a regular basis.

- While conclusions from packaged IIoT solutions may not be perfectly matched to your conclusions, experiment with these to get experience

IIoT Smarts
Science and Service

is AI constrained by your past?

What is happening? Our experiments with IIoT packaged solutions are going so well that even Overwhelmed Oscar can't seem to stop talking about their success. However, Reluctant Ruth, who's opinion, often sounded like an old chromogen, was highly respected. We need something more, an indicator that IIoT was not a passing fad and that it was here to stay. Our story continues with Irene and her daughter Izzy, a devoted college student.

Irene was beaming with pride this morning as she shared the conversation last night with her daughter Izzy. One of Izzy's college courses was to conduct research based on a handful of Harvard business studies. At a high level these studies were comparing organizations from three different approaches; keep doing what they're doing, accept change but only incrementally, focus on changing an industry by deliberately disrupting the status quo.

People were gathering as Irene began to play back the conversation. Mom, exclaimed Izzy, after listening to each bit of explanation on the three Harvard studies it was quite difficult to decide on which one was correct. The first example; "leave the business alone we are making money" made some excellent points, continued Izzy, however I really felt as though the rationale had much stronger value in the past and was not preparing organizations for our rapidly changing future. The second use case, "incremental change, slow and steady wins the race" certainly had its merits. However, it was easy to see that the reason for this approach had more to do with other factors such as bonuses and fear. Izzy paused for a minute and I couldn't tell what direction she was going to take, just then she burst out, "the third option of going all in and doing something very different was the most exciting for me". Irene remembered her goosebumps as she listened to the excitement in Izzy's voice.

Irene continued to share Izzy's story; our professor advised us to make sure that we looked at each of these three examples objectively, but that seemed next to impossible as the first two were just copout's. It was the final approach that seemed to make the most sense. Hey, if we were not surrounded by the convergence of sensors, data sciences, algorithms, and the ability to mash information up from multiple sources, maybe the other two had some merit. That simply was not the case in 2018. We can take advantage of information, leverage the science around what we were doing, and simply work smarter. There was no stopping Izzy now as she had incredible momentum, and as she continued explaining why science had to play a role for the business to survive, Irene was grinning from ear to ear. What a perfect moment.

The room was silent as Irene's work associates hung on every word, vicariously enjoying the pride Irene exuded from every ounce of her being. It wasn't just the story about Izzy and how others in the room had hoped to be able to share a story about their child one day, instead the room was filled with optimism that a generation entering the work force might not be saddled with the constraints that hold us back when contemplating innovation. We have all had conversations about green, sustainability, predictive modeling, and even some with prescriptive modeling. None of these are trivial tasks and the mass amount of effort to take your business from a traditional to a science-based environment takes one dose of technology and four doses of cultural change. IIoT systems will act like social networks, socializing connected product data to foster unparalleled knowledge and collaboration. When I see the future, summarized Irene, the reality that no product or asset will be an island, fills me with energy to keep pushing forward.

Moral:

Don't let your past paralyze your future (Greg Lush)

Start NOW:

- Decide which of the three represents you and your organization and plan accordingly, innovation is not for everyone

- While experience and intuition are important, decisions should be balanced with those without gray hair

- The impact science has on service is a worthy journey; however, will require a deliberate plan with lots of room for pivoting

IIoT Smarts
Choose a horse

commit to your IIoT platform quickly

Enough procrastinating! Looks like we have everybody on board, we understand the basics of what industrial IOT can deliver and we have a pretty good idea of how it will impact our customers and our business. So, the time has come for us to get together and determine which platform will launch us into the future.

Old Ollie reminisced about the days when we only had 13 channels of television in the United States. Roll the clock forward to 2018, and if you are within earshot of reluctant Ruth, you will hear her say time and time again, "thousands of TV stations and I still only watch five". It certainly is interesting when you think about it, major stations exist which feed 80% of what we want, however if we want to watch good American values we may tune in to the Hallmark Channel for those specific needs.

One is not better than the other, certain stations are focused in on our specific needs. For me, this is how I think about the Industrial Internet of Things (IIoT) and platform providers. Many niche providers will appear and disappear providing very specific functions. Yet there will be that 80% play, the one platform which you choose to aggregate these disparate systems and turn the IIoT data into action. I would predict that in the end, like the automotive industry, and communications industry, there will be a handful of platform providers which will dominate the market.

Seriously so that is your advice, thought overwhelmed Oscar. What exactly does that mean for me? How am I going to make any better decisions or narrow down the field of platform providers? Oscar, who had a wonderful relationship with Irene, decided to pose some of these questions to see what she had to say.... Irene listened intently as Oscar shared his thoughts laced with a heavy dose of fear. It seems to me Oscar, began Irene in a calm and soothing voice, that once you make a commitment to a platform you should probably stick with it. This reminds me of choosing a camera platform, leaders in the space are Canon, Nikon, Sony. When you choose a platform, say for instance Nikon, you have selected it because the features at that moment in time seem to appeal to you over the features of the other platforms. You realized, with few exceptions, that the platforms were relatively the same. For the type of photography, you would like to accomplish, how does the ecosystem of partners look for that platform?

As Irene continued to share examples, Oscar began to feel more comfortable. Irene, what I hear you saying is that the choice of platform needs to make sure that it can facilitate;

- long-term viability

- interconnections with other platforms

- ability to support broad ecosystems of sensors, actuators, data science tools, etc.

Fear is often the result of isolation and not knowing what lies ahead. This innate human feeling dictates many of our decisions. IIoT platforms are no different, fear is subconsciously driving your business decisions on which platform to select. Don't expect your decision to be perfect; however, when armed with objective inputs you should decide which will help you in the short and long-term. Irene could see the agreeing and nodding heads of Oscar and Ruth, which is a great start. Their real comfort will come from their industry, the use cases specific to them, and mapping the available ecosystem of partners to help them achieve their goals.

Moral:

Uncertainty will factor in to even the most confident of choices (Greg Lush)

Start NOW:

- The choice of platforms in 2018 is relatively simple as only a few can provide services holistic services. Partners such as: Microsoft, Amazon, Force, Google, GE

- A strong eco-system of partners is important as a solution will consist of many elements.

- Your ability to leverage solutions, platforms, learning model conclusions outside of your ecosystem is essential.

- Assess your short term and long-term use. Today, it seems like security is top of mind for most, however the reality is most providers offerings are still quite elementary.

Sea of Sensors

which to choose and how to prepare

Ruth may have been reluctant to start; however, now that a platform had been chosen she was fully engaged. This morning Overwhelmed Oscar came in to his office to find a box full of sensors and actuators. It seemed as if every shape, size, protocol, and output was included. A wave of anxiety swept across Oscar as he contemplated his next move. Oscar thought about a story shared with him just last week, it goes like this:

I awoke this morning, like any other morning, to my window shades automatically opening and the sound of Zip-a-Dee-Doo-Dah playing in the background. My coffee was brewing, and the micro heater was busy heating up just 10% over the average water volume I used over the last month for my shower. Then it happened, three screens within my house began displaying the news alert, rolling brown and black outs would affect your area today. What? This reminds me of the days when Enron was trying to fix market prices resulting in questionable power delivery, wasn't this all behind us? As I started eating breakfast, while fiercely peddling to keep my small generator running so I could see the latest news, another newsflash appeared stating that the brownouts were not real, this wasn't fake news but instead a shadow sensor. No sooner did I read the second announcement, the lights came back on. Things seem to have returned to the level of convenience I expect.

Even before I entered our office, filled with IIoT experts, I could hear naysayer Natalie saying, "we should only be deploying hardware encrypted sensors, see... this proves my case". While many of us would not disagree, it wasn't a luxury afforded to us in 2018. Chaotic Chris, who is normally pretty much ignored, had an excellent point as I entered the break room in our office. Chris continued, many of us, today and in the past, have hardened the gateway's and the connection to the cloud-based solutions. This makes sense and is straightforward. However, with IIoT we have a significant risk with the end points; sensors and actuators. The attack today had been inserting bogus data, subtly for a few months, disguised as a digital twin, let's say not the better half! By now most of the office was gathering, Chris was in his element and he continued with some end-point observations:

- hardware to hardware encryption is great (MCU), just limited at this time

- operating across the customers wireless network is not a very good move, keep networks separate

- smart edge devices, which can control essential functions are important, especially when they are designed to run without the Internet

Chris continued, we are all eager to jump in and get started with IoT. As this market matures more opportunities will reveal themselves, some with known players, and others with niche providers designed for very specific solutions. Proceed with caution and make sure, that at a minimum, the sensors/actuators you choose have a solid security model such as Microsoft Sphere or iterations of Blockchain. Andy was left speechless, astonished by the words coming from Chris's mouth. Truly relevant and inspired advice as we all explore this new frontier of industrial IOT.

Moral:

Be picky, informed, and deliberate; you have many choices. (Greg Lush)

Start NOW:

- Choose sensors that specifically match your requirements and pay close attention to the power consumption as changing batteries can eat up much of your automation savings

- Prepare your retrofit sensor packs to work in conjunction with other site visits such as service or PM

- Induction powered sensors are beginning to gain traction in the marketplace. Spending time selecting the proper sensor for short and long term is worth every minute.

- When leveraging existing sensors within control systems try to get as close to the actual sensor outputs as possible, sometimes downstream values will suffer from inexperienced programmers bias

Magnificent Models

what are you predicting?

Avid Andy opened this month's meeting with some great news sharing, "our IIoT endeavors are moving along nicely, we have seen a change in both our performance and the perception of our clients with regards to the service we deliver". After a moment of dramatic pause, Andy continued: it is now time to hunker down and get serious about how we were going to leverage the data collected from our field IoT devices. Enjoy the final story in our SMARTS with IIoT collection:

The next agenda topic in our executive meeting was IIoT and predictive service. Avid Andy had a feeling that this was going to be a controversial topic as there was a lot of ambiguity surrounding the definition of data science-based modeling. This was an opportunity to jump right in and start a brief discussion on the meaning and impact that data science-based learning models could have on the organization. He began by defining a couple distinct types of models:

The market today is filled with lots of misleading information, our competitors all say they can predict, we ourselves have manufacturers stating that they can also predict, and our customers have an expectation that we are predicting. My question is, predicting what? Aligned to which customer outcome? If we do not have a clear picture of all the elements, combined with the customer outcome all we will get are unintelligent responses such as your automobiles "check engine soon" light.

What level of confidence will you need from the predictive model? For instance, let's say that you were trying to predict when the air filters at any given jobsite are going to need to be replaced. Sounds relatively straightforward and the worst thing that would happen is that you may send somebody a bit too early or a bit too late. Another scenario might be when the battery needs to be changed in a pacemaker. The predictive algorithms and the confidence level that you are going to need to have in your outputs will need to be much higher on the replacement of the pacemaker battery. This all boils down to the level of investment on what your sensing and your expectations when leveraging that data.

Once you understand the customer's objective (s) you need to combine that with your own business objectives. Is the reason that you are using predictive modeling is to give you an edge in the market? If that is the case than the models that you choose should be single models, possibly only looking at one element and having the right to claim, rightly so, that you are predicting an outcome. However, if you are trying to turn around or mitigate risk within your organization, you may need to look at multiple pieces of equipment and their predictive models to see how, when combined with one another, create different perspectives which may alter your course of business. These are very different approaches, they all need predictive models and data, certainly investment, but their level of sophistication is vastly different. Both are valuable, the bottom line will be how well aligned the model is to your business conditions and environment.

The final thing to remember, don't shy away from collecting data, even the data which you may not see a direct use for today. This data is commonly stored in an inexpensive format often referred to as a data lake. If your ambitions are to mature your predictive models and evolve them eventually into prescriptive models, you will need all the data you can get your hands on. Andy was beginning to lose his team members in the executive meeting and decided to summarize using a few bullet points;

- grab as much data as you possibly can

- leverage other people's models to create a holistic model of your own which can align to customer outcomes

- start small with laser focus and understand your market and the models value

Learning models, and the algorithms contained within, can drive incredible value to your business. It is key that you understand how the outputs of these data science-based objects influence action with in your current operating environments. Keep in mind that IIoT, data sciences, and even workforce sciences, are less about the tools than they are about the cultural and market-based changes required to truly evolve your operation.

Moral:

Models are much more than skin deep, look carefully as choosing the right model (s) will impact your perspective (Greg Lush)

Start NOW:

- Translating what is in your head to a language that a data scientist can understand can be a bit challenging. Consider the use of stories to help communicate the intent of your requirements for your model

- Study and leverage available algorithms in the market, these algorithms can be bolted together to create spectacular solutions

- Do not shy away from collecting data even if you have no idea how to utilize it today

- Learning based models are the perfect vehicle to express your intuition and experience by transferring them into relevant action

Conclusion

When you think about it IoT is all around, from our coffee machines to automobiles, many are comfortable with the concept of reading a sensor and performing some automated action. I would ask you to consider the following analogy: do you want your IIoT efforts to be like a Tuba player or the Maestro of the Orchestra? While not speaking from experience, my thoughts are that playing one instrument, while beautiful on its own accord, is not as difficult as pulling all the instruments together to create the perfect harmony.

For years we have been Tuba players, concentrating on isolated systems. Sure, those of you familiar with process or building controls are saying; "no way" I have been making music for years. Consider not only thinking about a piece of industrial equipment and its complexity; but also, how that equipment ties to other elements within the plant, supply chain, product throughput, etc. We have been focused for many years around our spheres of influence, it is now time to expand that thinking, we have the data, the wherewithal, and the desire. Next time you look in the mirror, ask yourself; are you the Tuba player or the Maestro?

Intentionally left blank